Taking the Solo Out of Solopreneur

50 Tasks to Delegate So You Can Finally Claim Your Title of CEO

Kimberley Borgens

www.SoloToCEOMentor.com

Taking the Solo Out of Solopreneur

Published by:
90-Minute Books
302 Martinique Drive
Winter Haven, FL 33884
www.90minutebooks.com

Published in the United States of America

ISBN-13: 978-0692536377
ISBN-10: 069253637X

For more information on 90-Minute Books including finding out how you can
publish your own lead generating book, visit www.90minutebooks.com or call
(863) 318-0464

Here's What's Inside…

Forward

I grew up being told that if you want something, you have to do the work, and if you truly want it, then go get it yourself. Asking people to help was a sign of weakness. If you were weak, then you had little value in life. I decided to write this book on helping solopreneurs delegate because many solopreneurs like me think they have to become successful the hard way—by themselves. I want to help you, the solopreneur, understand the importance of letting people help you to become a success. Think about it: You once had an idea that turned into a vision, and you got passionate about it and then decided to start a business. What you didn't realize is that you have basically created your own job for yourself, even as you were trying to not have to work for a boss. Now you are the boss, the employee, the creative team, the account manager, and the sales and marketing team, too. You probably replaced a J-O-B for a job that sometimes feels like it is holding you hostage.

How do I know this? I was just like you: I wanted the freedom to be able to work my own hours, stay home with my kids, and have the flexibility to adjust my schedule as needed.

What I discovered along the way was that I worked 60 to 70 hours a week as an entrepreneur where I would have only worked 40 hours at a job. A job would have paid me to leave my work at the office and not take it home to my husband and children. As the solopreneur doing it all by myself, I was working while cuddling with my kids, making meals while talking to clients, and not getting enough sleep to be a happy spouse and parent. I often would ask myself, "Why, again, am I doing this?"

because even though the vision was clear, it really felt like trudging through mud with no energy.

Despite all that, there was no way I was going to ask for help! I was a woman who had to prove herself. I had to prove I could be a success and not let the naysayers win!

When my three-year-old son got sick with a rare disease, he needed more of my time dedicated to him. I still needed to be successful because now there were doctor bills and more time away from getting my work done.

I had to learn how to ask for help or I would have to go get a real job, and that would not help my son. I hired a part-time nanny to come into my home, so I could be there and work at the same time. I got my oldest son to do a few more chores around the house, and my husband stepped in where he could, but he was working graveyard shifts to keep our clients.

Once I had a little more time to work on the important things in business, I was able to get more done faster. We hired our first employee and started a team, so we could take on more clients. We were still working hard, but now, with help, we could do more. The next employee came along, and we could expand even more. Now, with over 100 employees, we have been able to maximize the impact to our community and get more done because more people are committed to the vision.

I was delighted to discover that the more that was delegated, the more the company could accomplish. I was finally able to do more of the things I wanted to do by starting a business. The freedom of setting my own hours (okay, *most* of the time), being able to stay home with the kids (although I was grateful when they went to school), and having the flexibility to do other things I wanted to do (not only the things I *needed* to do).

How do you know if this book is for you?

If you are working to build a profitable business, whether in a company you created, in a direct sales or network marketing business, or as an employee, this book is for you.

When you can understand what can be delegated and to whom and discover that you can accomplish more because you were willing to let go and let others help you, you will notice your business climbing up the success ladder. When you do that, you become the leader that your family has been waiting for you to be. You become the leader who leaves a lasting legacy for the lives that you touch, and you get to start claiming your chief executive officer role with a bigger vision and a greater impact in your community.

Why Don't More Solopreneurs Delegate?

The dictionary says that a **delegate** is someone you entrust (a task or responsibility) to, typically one who is less senior than oneself, someone you send or authorize to do something as a representative for you.

To delegate is the act of empowering or giving control, authority, a job, a duty, etc. to another person.

When you think about delegation, it is to assign responsibility or authority to someone else to complete agreed-upon tasks without giving up control of your business success. You entrust and empower people you have trained to act in your business as representatives of your good values, mission, and the vision of your company.

Why is it so hard to give away responsibility and/or authority to someone else?

Here are a few excuses I have heard from women on why they do not reach out and get the support they need and want.

Excuse #1: "I don't want to have to babysit."

When did you decide that you are your employee's mother? They don't need you to wipe their nose; they need you to lead and guide them. Tell them what you want done and when you want it done by. You can train them, or you can outsource the training. They can do it your way, or they can create new and more efficient ways to do the same things. Take your mothering hat off, and treat them like respectable adults, allowing them to step into leadership. When my clients work with me, they learn how to remove that mothering hat and put on their leadership hats, so they no longer feel like it is necessary to "babysit" those who are there to help them grow.

I have more than 100 employees, and I am grateful that they work for me. I look at employees as my way of giving back to my community. I am helping someone stay off the streets of homelessness. I am helping someone learn skills and job duties that, in some cases, can be used at home and in raising a family. By employing people, I help them feel good about themselves and, in some cases, stay off of government-regulated systems which tear down self-esteem and create depression. It may not make a big difference in the whole world, but it is a small difference that I get to make.

Excuse #2: "I can get it done faster because I know what I want."

How does it feel to know that you can get the little things done faster and ignore the really big things that you are meant to put your focus on? In order to grow your business in a way to live comfortably, travel, or do whatever else freedom looks like for you, you have to get help. Just because you are faster at something does not mean you are the one meant to do it.

I remember working with a particular client; when they hired me to facilitate and train people in personal development, they discovered I was very good at getting things organized. I created training manuals and organized systems to make the seminars run more efficiently so that, as facilitators, we would be more effective and not have to worry about the little things.

Along the way, they decided that I was so good at the little things that they began taking away the reason they had hired me in the first place: to facilitate. They put me into a box of what was fast and easy for me and not what I was meant to do. My true talent was being wasted because I could do something easier and faster. I ended up letting that client go because that is not the box I was meant to be in.

Excuse #3: "I don't have the time to train someone."

You're right! You don't have time to train people. Why would you? I am sure that the 30 minutes a day (or more) you are spending on social media will make you lots of money. Maybe it is because of all that time you spend out "networking" without ever really following up with the people you meet. Or that paper shuffling you keep doing on your desk without really getting anywhere with it is helping you make the money to support your family.

If something is truly important to us, we somehow seem to find the time to do it. It is not a glamourous job to train someone on new systems and skills to help you build a bigger business. When I hear this statement from clients, my internal knowledge rewrites it like this: "I am not organized enough to know the systems in my business to be able to train someone to work for me, and I don't want to look like an idiot."

That is why, when you work with me, you look good! Together we discover your little systems and your more complex systems, so you can learn to be an effective leader in business.

How Delegating Helps to Build Your Legacy

"I'm going from doing all of the work to having to delegate the work—which is almost harder for me than doing the work myself. I'm a lousy delegator, but I'm learning."
~Alton Brown, Chef and American TV personality

Are you ready to stop making excuses and build a thriving business that leaves a legacy?

Women often have a tendency to think that we have to do it all by ourselves! In reality, you do not get extra points in life for doing it on your own! You don't have to prove you can do it all. You only have to prove you are smart enough to get it done efficiently and effectively. Success truly comes when you learn to let go and let others help you!

What happens when you do not delegate? You become overworked. When people become overworked, they do not perform at their best. You are not able to give your clients the best of what you have. When you cannot give them your best, you are actually ripping your clients off because you are not making the space for yourself to truly be there for them. I know that you want to give them your best, and you often think that you are.

Just imagine for a minute the times when you have been upset because someone did not give you their best. If you told them about it, I am sure they would have said that they were giving you their best. It is not easy to see this in ourselves, and we would never want to think that we were not giving our best. Look at this another way: You are giving the best that you can in the moment; however, you may not realize that your best is not at 100%. In some cases you are likely only operating at 50% of your best because you are tired, overworked, and stressed, and your brain and body can only give out the level of energy that is available, and you have decided that it is your best.

Many of my clients say, "I don't know how to move from a solo business to a small business."

In order to grow into success, you have to be able to trust yourself to bring in the right people to help you, and you have to trust those people to get the important things done, which take the time constraints from you.

Most people believe that you can't grow until you are ready, and you can't be ready until you are making enough money to hire someone. The flaw in this thinking is that when you are making money, you are working, and you do not really have time to hire and train someone because you are so busy satisfying your clients. The best time to bring someone in and delegate is when you are not really ready for them.

I hired an assistant once because she was a friend and had been let go from a job she was not happy with. My heart truly wanted to be of service to her and her family, and I did not want her to be without a job, knowing her family situation. Don't get me wrong: I did not blindly hire her. I knew her skill level, and I told her that when she found a new position, I would not be offended when she left. I didn't need her at the time; however, I put her to work doing some typing for me. She also made phone calls I didn't want to do, and I was freed up to do more important things with my business.

Even though I wasn't ready for her, I made the right choice, took the risk, and made it easier for me. Plus, she was way better at the phone calls than I ever was. Quite often, I am seen as "mean, bossy, and arrogant" because I make quick decisions and I say "no" to people. The thing is, I know what I want my legacy to be, and I make choices from that space. I have a heart and a vison and mission to stay strong for.

By delegating a few things from my plate, I am able to sit down and write this book to support you. If I were still doing those things, then this book idea would still be shelved up in my mind, and you would not be reading it right now. It wasn't a lot that was taken off of my plate, but it was enough to be able to take the time to help you and leave a greater impact on my legacy.

As a business leader, you get the opportunity to leave a lasting legacy when you delegate. When you delegate to others, you help to develop the knowledge and skills of another human being. You build up the capabilities of each person working with you. In turn, they get to take that out into the world often in the form of confidence, courage, and knowing they are doing what they need to for their family. As you trust other people, you build trust in them as well. As you give them opportunities to grow, they develop new skills, and they get a chance to show you what they can do. They get to discover leadership in the process by watching you and by feeling they are important. This gets handed down to family, friends, and communities, and you make a bigger difference in the process.

Why Delegating Is Important for Growing Business

"If you really want to grow as an entrepreneur, you've got to learn to delegate."
~Sir Richard Branson, English businessman and investor

Have you ever wished you could clone yourself so you could get more done?

Delegating is a way to multiply yourself so you can get more done. When you delegate the things that you are no longer meant to do, it saves you time, increases your value as a business owner, and develops the people you get to help you.

Let's break this down:

1. Delegation saves you time.

    a. It is stressful when you have so much on your plate that you do not have the time to make sure you are making the right choices for your business. When you delegate some of the tasks, it frees up your time to think clearly, so you can make the best possible choices in the moment for your business growth. It is hard to make strong decisions when the workload you are carrying is heavy and stressful.

    b. When you delegate, you truly can get more done, and you are freed up to do the most important pieces of the business and your life, your vision, and your mission. This is what you created your business for in the first place.

2. Delegation increases your value.

    a. When you have help getting the tasks and job duties in your business completed in a timely manner, your clients appreciate their experience with you. When they appreciate you, they send referrals and are likely to buy again.

    b. Delegating allows you to be more efficient in business. When you delegate tasks to an employee/virtual assistant/helper, your job then becomes making sure that things get done without you having to do them. You increase your value because those are the people whose skills are better suited for the job, and that truly saves you money.

3. Delegation develops your team.

    a. When you build a team, it brings out the leader in you. You have important skills and abilities that you can pass on to others so they can help you grow your business. When you coach your team members in your skills, delegate the tasks that need to be done to them, and they use those skills, you have now created a legacy in your business. A good leader uses her time to go after what is truly important.

    b. When you build a team of people working alongside you, you gain credibility as a leader because you are leading. You also build respect and loyalty by giving people responsibility and holding them accountable for what you have delegated to them.

You can hire a virtual assistant for a specific project or task for a set number of hours. They will need to be interviewed to see if they can do what you need done. Find someone who has the time, skills, and understanding of what you want, so you get the most from their services. They usually have a set hourly rate, and they become a vendor for you.

You can hire an employee who you will need to train in your processes and systems. They will work on a multitude of tasks and/or projects and can probably even help to organize your thoughts and projects to get you moving more quickly. Whether you hire in-house employees or a virtual assistant, you are still freeing up your time to do more managerial work in your business, and that is really the key to greater business growth.

Have you ever thought about how much it costs to hire someone to help you?

I bet you are thinking that it is going to cost you a lot of money. You are thinking, "I can't afford to hire someone to work for me."

If you start small and hire someone for 10 hours a week or 40 hours a month at $10 an hour, it will cost you about $500 a month. No, my math is not off! The $400 you pay in payroll, and then 25% more, covers employee taxes, workers' compensation, and insurance. I am sure you are running through your head the idea that you cannot afford to pay out $500 a month when the truth is, if you want to grow your business, you can't afford not to.

Think about the time-wasting activities you are currently doing. If these were given to someone else, you would have the opportunity to put your focus on getting new clients. New clients equal more money for your business and, in turn, pay for the support of an employee.

I know a lot of people who are willing to invest thousands of dollars into the next training program for sales, coaching, personal development, and mastermind programs but who are not willing to invest in an employee who will actually help them implement all of the trainings in which they have already invested and are not using.

What if you went around your house and took inventory of all the things you are no longer using? Could you have a yard sale, put some things on eBay, Craigslist, or sell them to your Facebook friends? Could you imagine getting some things uncluttered to be able to hire someone who can keep you more organized and focused?

If you stopped going out to eat for a month (including that special coffee stop), how much money would you save each month? You may have to sacrifice a bit to be able to get someone to come in and help you increase your value as a businessperson.

When my clients begin working on their Solo to CEO Blueprint, we start with a five-week virtual training program in which I help them discover the specific things to delegate and the systems to make that easy to do. Then they discover the Three Secrets to Planning a Team, finding the right interviewing process for them, what and how to train to get the best out of their team, and what to do when it is not working out. Once they discover what to delegate, we create a plan to get it delegated to the right people, and they can grow to a more profitable business.

The Three Starting Steps to Delegating with No Pain

Step 1: Make a list of everything you do in a day/week/month.

- Write down everything you do on a regular or daily basis.

- What are the things you really get excited to do? Circle those things on your list.

- What are the things that completely drain you or that you wish you did not have to do? Highlight those items on your list.

- What is left?

Most likely, the things you circled are the things for which you started your business. It is likely these are not yet ready to be delegated to someone else. (You will be able to determine this by the end of this book.)

The things you highlighted are likely those for you to create a plan to delegate.

The key is to know exactly what you need or want to get help with, so you will know what to say when you bringing in your support team. Whether you are hiring an employee or a virtual assistant, you want to get the biggest bang for your buck by knowing what you are asking for and how quickly you need it done. So many entrepreneurs will go to someone and say something like, "I know I need help, but I just do not know with what." This usually ends up costing you more money because people are spending time trying to figure it out for you, and you are paying them.

Think of this list process as you get to learn where your strengths and weaknesses are, and that will give you feedback on what you could use your time to learn and what not to spend time on in the future.

Step 2: Develop your plan to delegate.

In order to create the plan, you will want to answer these questions:

- What is the item or task you will delegate?

- How much training will it need?

- How long does it normally take you to complete?

- Why is this task important to your company?

- Why is this task important to the client?

- If anything, what is the benefit to them for completing the task?

Step 3: Find the right people for the right tasks.

Finding people who are naturally good at the tasks you want help with is a big win. They make it easy, and because of that, they are not going to spend a lot of time trying to figure it out. They feel the task and take it on because it is a right fit for them. Whether you are getting help from an intern, a virtual assistant, or a new employee, you want to make sure you find the right person for the job. Once you have found the person, you must communicate clearly and have a communication plan in place, so they can communicate with you.

If you can, it is best to meet with people face-to-face to evaluate if you are the right fit for them and if they are the right fit for you. If they are a virtual assistant, use Skype or video chat of some form to speak face-to-face.

Tell the person why they were selected for this task and what results you expect from them. How will they know when the task or assignment is complete? Encourage them to ask you questions. What is the expected outcome for completion? Have them share back with you what they understand this assignment to be. You could say, "I want to make sure I have communicated effectively what I need. Share with me what you have heard so far" to keep them from getting defensive or feeling like you do not think they are capable of success.

The reality is that you are bringing people in to produce results for you and your clients (both current and future).

Does Delegating Make You a CEO?

"I think one of my strengths is that I can always take advice, and I can delegate. I know a lot of people feel the need to do everything themselves, but I am not one of them."
~Dasha Zhukova, Russian businesswoman and magazine editor

With this book, my goal is to help you see that delegating some of your business tasks out to others can free you up to do the more important things that a chief executive officer would spend their time doing. Anyone can be a solo entrepreneur, but to become a CEO, the first step is to start to think like one and get other people to work for you.

Delegating is only one step to becoming the successful businesswoman that you want to be. Without delegating to an employee, a virtual assistant, an intern, or even trading services with another businesswoman, you are likely going to find yourself in a place where you make $25,000 to $75,000 or less a year and be comfortable with that. You can live decently off of it, so why grow? What happens when the economy tanks, and your clients begin to fade away? What happens when an emergency suddenly arises, and you are stressed because you cannot work in the time of crisis?

I am so very grateful for having a successful and thriving corporation. Even as a CEO of my own company, when my dad died after a very short battle with leukemia, I did not want to work. I wanted to reflect and truly take notice of this man who came into my life as a teen. I was able to give myself permission to take the necessary time off because I had a team of people in place to keep the business going. I have a very supportive spouse and partner, and he loved me through this time, knowing I would jump back in. We each had faith in the team to pick up my slack.

When it is important to have time off if you are a "one-stop shop," so to speak, you cannot afford to take time off. You end up frustrated and, in some cases, angry because of the self-imposed job that you created, and you struggle to find the freedom that you originally created your business to be.

"Leadership is about making others better as a result of your presence and making sure that impact lasts in your absence. You want to make the company better, and leave it that way for your successor. That should be the goal of any executive."
~Sheryl Sandberg, COO of Facebook

Are You Waiting
for Permission
to Be Successful?

= Granted =

Now Go Do it !

Kimberley's Top 10 Things to Delegate for Beginners

I want to make it easy for you to get started on delegating. I chose these 10 items to get you started on the journey to delegating because they are simple to train, often easy to let go of, and can begin to free up a little bit of your time, so you can do more of the important things in your business. Many of these items are easy to ask someone to do versus putting a lot of time into training first. They are in no particular order, and some may not even apply to you based on where you are in your business journey. Pick one, and get started. Make it simple, and then add another to your assistant/virtual assistant/intern job duties, and take a look at where your time could be spent to create more value.

1. Answer phone calls

2. Create your newsletter

3. File, organize, and type your notes

4. Fulfill product and service orders

5. Open and sort mail

6. Research product and services ideas

7. Send notes and cards (anniversary, birthday, celebration, holiday, sympathy, thank you, thinking of you, etc.)

8. Schedule appointments for your calendar

9. Update contacts and CRM

10. Call contacts to fill your events (mixer, party, open-house, training, product launch, board

meeting, customer appreciation, retreat, team-building, business dinner, seminar, charity)

When you delegate, you empower others to step into their own leadership. You let them become involved and take a personal interest in developing and growing your business with you. You enable them to grow their confidence in their skills, knowledge, and capabilities. You are giving gifts to your community of support. They learn and grow because you believed in them and they stepped up to it.

One of the largest pieces of delegating is communicating the importance of the tasks that you have assigned. Often, the employee gets your list of tasks and will do them, but they do not necessarily put your values or their heart and soul into the tasks as they complete them. When you communicate why certain tasks are important to the success of the company and to their own success in the company, they see the benefits and are likely to take on the tasks as important.

You also have to let them know how much authority they have in the tasks. What can they act on? Can they make the decisions necessary to complete the tasks at hand? Is there anyone who needs to know that you have given them the authority to act for the completion of certain projects? Discuss this with them, so the boundaries are clear for them, for you, and for anyone else who may need to be involved.

How Your Role Evolves When You Delegate

"The way you delegate is that first you have to hire people that you really have confidence in. You won't truly let those people feel a sense of autonomy if you don't have confidence in them."
~Robert Pozen, American financial executive

Once you have delegated the tasks and duties, then you get to let them go and let someone else handle them. Your job becomes to train, supervise, observe, review, and guide that person to completion. You basically get to inspect what you expect. Confirm that it is on track or has been completed, observe that you trained them properly, and review the completed task.

Once you delegate, you have to make sure to be open to their coming to you and talking about the task. They may need to get some clarity or ideas, and you will have to make sure you do not take the task back. This is your opportunity to coach them and guide them. If they are unsure of how to do something, ask them what they would do if they were making the decision. What kind of training do they feel they need to complete this task? Listen without judgement, and use the opportunity to train them further, if necessary.

By doing this, you help them be a problem-solver for you and your business in the future. When you create people who can solve problems, they take ownership of their space in your company. They often work better because they can do things without needing you to figure them out for them.

Isn't that the reason you really want to pay someone, to have the confidence to help you and be a valuable part of the team?

It is important to ask yourself a few questions to help you see how useful delegating is and to take away some of the guilt you might have for not doing everything in your business.

- How can I give up some responsibility to someone else?

    o Who else is capable of doing this task?

    o Who has the time to complete this task?

    o What are the results I want to accomplish by giving this task away?

    o Who has the skill or experience to accept the responsibility of this task?

- Did I communicate clearly what is being asked of the person?

    o Have them share back what they heard you say.

    o Ask for ideas on how they see this project getting completed.

    o Who else might need to be involved in the project?

    o Is there a completion time/date? How will progress be communicated and monitored?

- What can I do to support and encourage my support team?

    o Discover who needs to learn how to handle more responsibility on your team, and then give them opportunities to step up.

- o Ask yourself if the person needs training or guidance to complete the task or action.

- o Let them know who else might be able to support them in the process.

- o Provide feedback of what worked, what didn't work, and what's next.

Remember, you are not abandoning the tasks and jobs in your business. You are handing them off to someone else in order to multiply yourself. You will always be responsible for them. You get to assign your team the responsibility of achieving the necessary results. You are not dumping tasks onto people. You get to build them up, build confidence, and encourage results for the greater good of the company.

It is also your job to discover what was learned from the process of delegation. What did the employee learn from what they took on? What did you learn in the process? How can you utilize what you both have learned from this process? Does this information need to be implemented or shared with other team members? Does this information need to be added to a training manual for future support?

Don't Focus on Perfection, Focus on Leverage

"If you want to do a few small things right, do them yourself. If you want to do great things and make a big impact, learn to delegate."
~John Maxwell, American author and speaker

Are you a recovering perfectionist like me? Perfection seems to get in the way of a lot of women entrepreneurs. Because you are not ready, it is not perfect, it could be better, and all of the other reasons you hold yourself back in business, you are really creating the space to fail versus ever really getting out there to be a success. It seems like the norm to be a failure to ourselves rather than allow other people see us make mistakes. The bigger issue is that it is unrealistic to think that anything about being in business should be perfect.

A few things that hold someone with a perfectionist mindset back and what clients have actually said to me include:

- Never getting started—"It will never be perfect."

- Their way is the only way—"No one can do it as well as I can."

- Procrastination—"I waited so long that someone else made the decision for me."

- Always focusing on the mistakes they made—"I am not willing to take the risk."

What if you could let other people help you become even more successful? Have you thought that when you hire someone to help you, you are actually leveraging your time, money, and energy? You end up getting more "bang for your buck," so to speak, because you can accomplish more with the help of others.

Business is messy, ugly, uncomfortable, and downright scary! I know I am able to help so many more people as a business consultant because of the ugly, messy, and scary stuff I have experienced. When I share about some of the hardest and messed up things in business that I have learned from or have overcome, people actually have more respect for me and it builds my credibility as a businesswoman. People want to know that successful women are human and make mistakes and have still find ways to be successful.

Have you noticed that successful business leaders all have people working for them?

Imagine you were to hire someone to make appointments for you, address and stamp your cards, send out your packets, respond to emails, and answer incoming phone calls. How much would you be willing to pay them to do the simple tasks? Minimum wage? Double minimum wage?

Think about it another way. If you were like me and charged for your services—let's say your client paid you $100 per hour for your services—would you be willing to pay someone the same $100 to make your appointments, mail your packets, and so on? It is not likely that you would be willing to pay that price for those simple tasks, but that is exactly what you are doing by doing those tasks for yourself. You are paying a price that is equal to what you could be paid for that time. By not leveraging support, you are actually costing yourself more than if you were to delegate those tasks. You get to leverage your time by taking only those calls that could turn into paying clients.

An assistant can take calls to answer frequently asked questions as well as spending those few minutes with the people who are calling just to pick your brain. Your assistant can let people know the details of your next upcoming event, draft emails for you, set up webinars and video conferencing, and create and complete forms for your business. When they do these things for you, you are actually leveraging your time and money for the betterment of your business. You get to put your focus on your strengths, and they, in turn, get to do the same for you. When you find the right people who have the right strengths based on what you choose to delegate, you build a more confident and energized team, which creates much better results than you ever could on your own.

"Surround yourself with the best people you can find, delegate authority, and don't interfere as long as the policy you've decided upon is being carried out."
~Ronald Reagan, American actor, politician, and 40th President of the United States

The Three Things You Should Never Delegate

1. You really cannot delegate your vision for your company, the values you hold for your business, or your mission. These items are for you to retain and keep close to your heart. You can inspire people to support and walk alongside you in your vision, mission, and values, but you are ultimately responsible for keeping your company and staff on track in terms of how they're enacted.

2. You cannot delegate the ultimate responsibility of your business unless you sell it or close it down. You are the responsible party for your business! If you are successful, it's your fault. If you are not successful, it is, again, all your fault. If things go well, you praise your support team. If things do not go well, it is all on you. Take the responsibility to discover where you might have missed something which could have prevented a problem or an issue, be it in training, hiring the right people, or under-delivering on a promise.

3. You are the key driver in your business. It is up to you to keep control of the reins in your business. You are in charge of the ideas, the systems, the programs, the policies, and the jobs in your business. You can delegate responsibilities to a manager and know you still must inspect what you expect from them. Do not give up control of something and walk away like it no longer matters. You

always want to know how everything gets done in your company. You want to make sure that everyone knows why they are doing the jobs they have in your company. Have you ever heard the saying, "Those who know how work for those who know why?" You always want to stay close to your why and keep reminding your support team.

Still Not Ready to Delegate?

"Deciding what not to do is as important as deciding what to do."
~Jessica Jackley, American businesswoman and Co-Founder of KIVA

By now, I hope you have been able to determine what in your business you can easily delegate and what you really should do for yourself.

Remember, delegating does not have to be hard! It is actually much harder in our thinking than it is in reality.

Not everyone is meant to be an entrepreneur. Believe it or not, there are only a small number of women leaders out there. Most people prefer to be employees. These great people are the doers and taskmasters who support business leaders in growing their businesses. I am grateful for those who are willing to work for and with me. Without them I know I would not be able to make the impact in the world that I am meant to make. I would not be making the money to impact more people around me to live out the legacy I want to leave. I have actually done more good in my community and my world by hiring people to help and support me than if I tried to do it alone.

If you are sitting there still thinking that you are not ready or cannot afford to hire someone to help you grow your business, then reach out and ask for a strategy session to see if there is something in the tool chest to help you move forward in your journey to becoming a CEO. Visit our website, www.SoloToCeoMentor.com, to find upcoming events, tips, and tools to help you prepare to build your Solo to CEO Blueprint and stop being the best-kept secret in your business field.

"It has been so hard to get away. Remind me again why it took so long to hire someone!"

Here Is the Creating Your Business Success Team Blueprint

When it comes to growing a successful money making business delegating is one of the key secrets to success. It is not easy to give away the pieces of "your baby" you call business. You have nurtured it from the beginning and cared more than anyone else. When you are delegating out the tasks to others it is like sending your child off to school. You let the task go because the training and learning you are providing for your business is essential for it to grow into the blessing you know you are to bring to the world around you. To help you make the transition from solopreneur to becoming your business CEO we have created the **Creating Your Business Success Team Blueprint** a virtual training that gives you the three secrets to planning a team, success strategies for training your team, recruiting, interviewing techniques, how to keep your team and what to do when it is not working. I have outlined the five steps below in the Creating Your Business Success Team Blueprint so you can clearly understand how to start to finally claim your title of CEO.

As I walk you through these five steps you will see how delegating plays a key part in building a successful business team for you and your business. You will discover the progression of determining your tasks and systems, developing a culture for your company, designing your hiring system, establishing a pleasant work environment and what to do when it is not working. As you read through these steps you can see the progression of bringing together a team so you can take the solo out of being a solopreneur.

Step 1 – 3 Secrets to Planning a Team

The first secret is to discover is the tasks you can delegate. Using the list included in this book to help you get started. The second secret is to make a list of five to ten tasks that you can see yourself getting started with so you can get someone to help you grow your business. Now that you have made your list, the third secret is to take each item and begin to design a system to complete each task. Write down all the steps it takes for you to get the task completed. The smallest to the largest things you do to complete any given task in your business.

I know these three secrets are not everyone's favorite thing to do. That is why you are still doing business for yourself. This is the hard work necessary to creating an easier life! Here is an example to help you see how to create a system for your task.

Example: Task – Filling Meeting/Training with Attendees

- Get together a potential attendee list

- Update and print out list

- Send an email to let them know someone will be reaching out to contact them

- Create a script of how the call will go

- Create a list of frequently asked question and answers

- Create a message for leaving a voice mail

- What is the "call to action" information

  o Direct to webpage/landing page

  o Take payment on the phone

- Follow Up – What is the next step

  o Add to call back list

  o Add to event attendees

  o Send an "I'm glad you made a choice" email to those not attending

  o Get more potential attendees and repeat the process

Some of these seem too simple yet by having the simple steps laid out you can easily train people and break it down to make sense especially if they are brand new to your industry and ideas.

In order to move toward training people to do what you have been doing you must have a system in place as a tool to grow. As a solopreneur you can *"wing it"* for a long time by just doing what you know. It becomes common sense to you. As you work with people occasionally you may forget a piece of your process. You had a tough phone call or you were really excited about someone taking a next step so you missed a piece of your normal process and you can dismiss that piece because it worked for you in that moment.

The challenge comes when you hire someone to work for you and because you are *"winging it"* with them they do not create the same results as you and then you begin saying to yourself "this is not working" or "I am losing money with and employee". You will be right on both accounts, but it won't be because the person you hired is at fault. It will be because you did not have an easy and complete system for them to follow in place. When it comes to creating a system, the little things matter.

Step 2 – Creating Your Success Team Strategies

During the five week Creating Your Business Success Team Blueprint virtual program I work with my clients on setting up the success strategies to not be taken advantage of and how to get the most out of the money and time you are putting into your business. Setting up clear expectation with the people you work with is important for both sides to win. This is one of the reasons I am known as the **"Queen of Accountability"** because you can't hold people accountable if they do not even know your expectations. Many times women have unspoken expectations and then have their feelings hurt because the other person did not know what the expectation was and clearly missed the invisible mark. Taking away the invisible ink to create your business strategies is a big win for you and those you work with.

In this step we talk about setting the boundaries in your business so it is clear to see what is expected and what happens when these are overstepped. Having that in place takes away the need to "babysit" as I spoke about in the chapter about why solopreneurs don't claim their title. If you discover what your boundaries are and where the line is in business you can make faster choices based on those boundaries.

Between setting clear expectations, knowing your business boundaries and having a clear communications plan the people that work with you will feel empowered, less annoyed when a system changes or a challenge arises because they know what is going on and that is a much more efficient way to do business.

When a client of mine was doing everything on her own and she had no boundaries set up she was getting taken advantage of. She would do extra hours on her client's behalf because they kept piling more onto her because she would let them get away with it. She didn't charge them more money for all the extra hours she was putting in because she didn't want to lose what money she was making. She also didn't want to tell the client no because she needed the income to survive. I helped her put a stop to that! She gained confidence to say no to giving away more work than the original agreement stated without more pay. She set boundaries with the clients that were taking advantage of her. When one client decided that they would go somewhere else for similar services because they could no longer take advantage of her, she already had a systems and new clients in place to replace that lost income and time. In the Creating Your Business Success Team Blueprint some of the strategies are there to help you set boundaries and create the necessary structures to help you release the people who are really not the right fit for your business and that alone creates wonderful freedom of who you work with.

Step 3 – Simplifying Your Interview System

You have your tasks set aside, your systems created and now it's time to hire your first team member. It's time for you to take a risk and begin hiring people to work for you. In this step we help you discover how to find the people to fit into your position. Did you know there are multiple ways to interview people? We go over the **Five Ways to Interview** so you maximize your time, energy and resources. Where do you find people and how do you design a job description? We have that covered too. We help you take the guess work out of bringing in people to help you delegate.

In this process we work with you to create a job description that is fun, honest and lets people know what you want from them if they decide to interview with you. We help you find the places to put your job description to recruit the best team for you and them I walk you through choosing the right interview process for what you want to accomplish.

When you get into hiring people it is kind of like going out on a first date. It is your job to sell yourself in such a way that someone else is interested in discovering if you are the right fit for them. The interviewing process is really like a deselection process. An interview is where you tell them your vision, your mission and your values and then you both get to decide if you want to go further (like making a second date). As you both progress in the process you both continue to make decisions on going on to the next step.

As a business woman you want to share who you are, what your company is about, what is important to you in your business, what your company culture is and what you expect from them if they are hired. If they are the right fit based on what is in the job description and what you know you want to create in the future then you get to make an offer to bring them into the team. For many people this step is a hard one for them. You want to hire someone so you can make money and you don't want to spend the money to hire someone because you are uncertain it will work out and that money will be gone. Having the system to hire and interview helps you find the right people to bring into your company so you can begin claiming your CEO title.

Think about your cost of building your business without support. Coming from where you are right now, does the guilt show up because you cannot seem to find the time or energy to spend quality time with your loved ones? How much stress are you putting on yourself and your family to do all the work yourself? Are you turning away work or opportunities because it feels overwhelming to do something new? By putting the right systems and people in place you can get back to the reason you built a business and spend the right time and energy with the most important pieces of your life.

Step 4 – Preserving Your Success Team

You have hired your first employee, they are ready to jump in and help you out and you are thinking now what! I shared in step 1 how to create a system for your tasks to delegate to help you create a training plan. This training plan will help to make it easy for you to show your new assistant what is important and how to do what you need done. Now the question is "How do you keep them". Often people decide to work with you not because of the money but more importantly because they want what you have. They want to help your vision, they want to support your mission and they can be excited about what you are creating. It will be your job to keep them connected to your vision, mission and values in an environment that makes people want to come to work for your everyday.

The first step after hiring is to welcome them into your company. Make them feel welcomed. Do you have a place for them to work? How many hours and what schedule will you two be working within? Are you organized enough to have the place and tools available for them to be a success. Of course get all the paperwork done to satisfy the laws and requirements and welcome them with arms open wide.

Invite them in, share about your company culture, why it is important and ask them if they have any question about that. I let my team know that they can ask any question because I believe there are no stupid questions and most often mistakes happen because of unasked questions. That is part of my culture. I let them know that when they ask a question I will not dismiss it, belittle it or make them feel guilty for asking it. I want people to feel like they can ask me questions and not feel like they are bothering me which reduces the possibility of them making a mistake. I also share that I have a strong drive, I get a little more "bold" (okay I can be bossy sometimes) than most and I will hold them accountable for the job I ask them to do. I then let them share with me what kind of culture they would like to work in. It will be give and take as we work together so I want to know what it takes for them to get committed to working on my team.

Next step for a new hire is to train them. I have a binder for my assistant that has a list of all the tasks, a description of each task and the system that was created for each task neatly put together in one place. Why would I do this? Let's get this cleared up now - you do not have to be the most organized person to be able to do this. You pick up a binder and have it where your assistant can get to it and you utilize this as your training manual. When you join the **Solo to CEO University** you will go deep on creating a training manual that is always available for updates, new tasks and description because having an organized training manual saves you time, energy and money! For now we are only talking the basics of a binder for you to efficiently train a new person on your business needs.

You then walk them through each task, description, and then go over all the pieces of the system. Have them take notes, even if they do not want to take notes, let them know taking notes is required for the job. (*I hope you are asking yourself right now why I would suggest that. The answer is by having them write it down it actually creates memory in the brain. When people take the action while you are talking it helps them learn. I want my team to learn what I am teaching them so I have them take notes. They will learn more effectively with writing and repetition.*) After you complete one task then ask them if they have any questions. If they do, then answer their questions to clear up confusion. Remember they are not questioning you the boss, they are questioning the system. You as the boss are the representative for the system. Get your ego out of the way and focus on the greater results the questions can bring to your company.

Once the questions are complete then have them teach you about what they just learned as if they were training a new hire. Sounds a little crazy I know because they haven't even done the task yet. By doing this you get to see how their listening skills are and any points you may have missed in the training process. You just listen and take notes for their observations and what may need more training on. Once that is complete make the necessary adjustment to the training and proceed to the next task. Keep going until you have gone over all the tasks you are delegating. The next step would be the hands on part of the training. This process may take a couple hours to a couple of days. It will be worth it in the end.

Lastly, you want to make sure that you and your assistant are clear of the boundaries of employer and employee. You are not there in this position to be their friend! You must remain in the mind of an employer and make it personable yet not personal. If it doesn't work out as the employer/employee position you will have to let them go. You do not want to lose your best friend because you had to fire them.

We had an employee that worked for us and we worked together on a lot of things in the business. She trusted enough to share her family stories and about her life in general. She worked for us for several years. She and another employee in our company created a relationship and decided to marry. She came to me and asked if I would be her maid of honor for her wedding. I was honored to be asked and I declined the offer. I let her know that as much as I like and appreciate her, I did not feel it was in both of ours best interest. A few years later I had to fire both of them for embezzling from my company. I knew then and I know now that I had made the right choice to be personable with employees without being personal with them. Keeping a professional relationship with those you hire is important and it is a lot easier on the heart too.

Speaking of the heart, how wonderful would it be to get back to doing the things you love to do in your business verses the tasks that are necessary to do in your business? That is why you started in business to begin with right? While you are **Creating Your Business Success Team Blueprint** you will learn how to make training people easy because you will have the systems in place to do so. When you can duplicate yourself it takes the guess work out of hiring the right people necessary so you can do what you love. And your business will grow in the process.

How many times have you tried to reinvent the wheel in your business so far? "If I could just come up with the right thing I would have more clients"! This is the kind of thinking that puts solopreneurs out of business. If you take what you already know, create an effective system to use it, add a few tweaks here and there and bring in the right help you would be able to grow your business. This is the reason I train clients in building a long term **Solo to CEO Success Plan**. I help clients put the right systems in place to be effective and efficient. By teaching you to train someone and help you stick to what you love to do, you create more in business. You begin to think like a Chief Executive Officer and you begin to see the benefits of your consistency paying off. Many of my clients will invest deeper and schedule a **VIP Day** with me to help specifically nail down the systems and training in a day to get them started right away because they are ready to not waste any more time preparing and are ready to take action. If this is you go to our website **www.SoloToCEOMentor.com** to get an application.

Step 5 – What To Do When It's Not Working

The last step of the Creating Your Business Success Team Blueprint is on what to do when it is not working out with your assistant. Not always the topic people want to talk about. Actually because most people do not want to talk about this step it often ends up costing them more money, time and frustration than necessary. When is it time to fire?

If you are finding yourself frustrated and feeling like you are wasting money the first thing you have to ask yourself is *"is it the person or the system?"* If it is not working out is it because the person is unwilling to do the job required or they are unable to do the job required? You can check this to see which is the really the issue before you let someone go. If the person in unwilling to do the job because they do not like it, they are confused or they can't

40

see the vision of your company then it would be time to let them go. If they are unable to do the job because they have been improperly trained, they do not have the work space necessary, they do not have the tools or resources to do the job or you have created an unfriendly work environment then that is on you. You can choose to course correct any of the issues that make them unable to the job and then move forward from there.

Maybe you have a policy like we do called *"Believe or Leave"* where we ask our employees to believe in the company vision, mission and values and at any time they feel they cannot believe in those pieces then they are welcome to leave or they will be asked to leave. Our bottom line is that we want people to be satisfied in their life and enjoy what they are doing. If they are not enjoying working for us and they are so unsatisfied in their job then we want them to go someplace where they can get that for themselves. We work hard to create safe communities and part of safety is the attitude of those around you.

Lastly, you have to let go of the emotions that you may have of terminating someone from your employment. **This is a business decision!** Your business has a culture but it does not have emotions. Let people know that you are letting them go because it is not working out for the company and wish them well. There is no need to bring up what didn't work with them. It is a clean and clear decision due to it not working the way you and the company need it to work and let them know something that you did appreciate about them. Maybe something like "I really appreciated that you were on time to work every day". I wish you the best in finding your next position. Then let it go. When you continue to pay someone who is not the best fit for your company you are rewarding them and taking away from your company and ultimately your family. When you misplace reward by keeping people who are not working out, then you devalue those people who are doing a great job for you. When you devalue results it causes frustration to the other people working with you and they will seek out employment or services elsewhere. When you reward those for not working out and devalue those who want to support your vision there is a disconnection in your company. Other employees will notice the little results the employee who is not the right fit creates and they decide they too will only give you what is necessary to do the job and therefore not giving you their best. **Don't pay people for just showing up at your business**. Pay them because they are an asset to your vision, your mission and your clients.

Remember delegating does not have to be hard! It is much harder in our thinking than it actually is in reality. Not everyone is meant to be an entrepreneur. Believe it or not, there are only a small number of women leaders out there. Most people prefer to be employees. These great people are the doers and tasks masters who support business leaders to grow their businesses. I am grateful for those who are willing to work for and with me. Without them I know I would not be able to make the impact in the world that I am meant to make. I would not be making the money to impact more people around me and to live out the legacy I want to leave. I have actually done more good in my community and my world by hiring people to help and support me than if I tried to do it alone.

Here's How to Get Started on Creating Your Business Success Team

Are you still saying to yourself "I can't afford to hire someone" to delegate to? If you want to grow your business to where you have the flexibility to adjust your schedule and spend more time with higher paying clients then really you cannot afford not to hire someone to help you in your business. Imagine how it would feel when you create your dream team of people to help you in business so you can position yourself to finally claim your title as CEO.

The **5 Steps to Creating Your Business Success Team Blueprint** is the tool you need to grow your business. As an entrepreneur you have worked so long without a lot of resources to grow and you are used to doing it alone. This program helps you build up your access to more resources so you can be in business for yourself but not by yourself!

When you sign up for the program we begin by assessing what you already have and what you still need to create the success team to grow in business. There is a questionnaire, a private group of participants and all the training to get you ready to say yes to growing your business with a team. As a bonus for going through the virtual program you will receive an opportunity to come train with me live, which can be a lot of fun and you can dig in deeper with me for your specific needs.

The entire package of the 5 Steps to Creating Your Business Success Team Blueprint is worth over $5000 and you can get access to this program right now for just $997 or 3 easy payments of $397. Yes you can buy the 5 Steps to Creating Your Business Success Team Blueprint online anytime for $1997, but right now, for trusting yourself and taking fast action, you save $1000. Just visit www.SoloToCEOMentor.com/fastaction right now and you will begin enjoying our course pre-work to get you started.

Can you begin putting your trust in finding the right systems and people to finally claim your title as CEO? If you do not do this now, you are likely going to continue doing business the way you always have. Leaving yourself to do all the work and creating more stress for yourself and your family. You will continue to miss out on the activities your heart wants you to do and do what you have to in business to scrape by each month.

Decide today that you are ready to make the shift from solopreneur to the CEO leader you are meant to be in business.

If you are interested is stepping up, all you need to do to get started is to visit us at www.SoloToCEOMentor.com/fastaction and get enrolled in the next program. It's simple, quick and easy to get started. And, what better time than now to get your business to the place it needs to be to make the impact you were meant to make in the world

Thank you for taking the time to honor yourself with these gifts. I hope you will take these tools and make quicker decisions in your business to the opportunities that present themselves to you. That you will see the benefits of these steps and get the support and help to be able to enjoy your life more fully.

You have stepped out and became a solopreneur and you deserve to make a bigger impact with your skills and knowledge. You deserve peace of mind and to enjoy the benefits that truly comes with being an entrepreneur.

Fifty Things You Can Delegate

1. Answering frequently asked questions

2. Attending networking meetings on your behalf

3. Booking guests for tele-summits and tele-seminars

4. Booking speaking engagements, radio shows, and interviews

5. Bookkeeping—Maintaining financial records for P&L, receipts, paying the bills (You still sign checks.)

6. Screening calls and answering phones

7. Confirming scheduled engagements

8. Repurposing content

9. Coordinating networking events

10. Copywriting sales pages, webpages, and newsletters

11. Creating press releases, press release kits, and mailers

12. Creating procedure and job description manuals, assembling information packets

13. Creating timelines—Events, projects, launches

14. Creating opt-in boxes, websites, tele-classes, webinars, and special promotions

15. Creating surveys and questionnaires

16. Doing creative design and ordering for business cards, brochures, and flyers

17. Data entry—Contacts and CRM info

18. Designing e-books and home study materials

19. Designing PowerPoint presentations

20. Educational guides, workbooks, e-books

21. Making follow-up calls

22. Gathering testimonials

23. Giving information for products and services

24. Housekeeping, grocery shopping, and laundry

25. Invoicing clients

26. Keeping things in good working order—phones, computers, etc.

27. Listening to meeting audio and creating meeting notes

28. Making phone calls to fill events

29. Managing sponsors and support services

30. Meeting minutes—Creation, distribution, and filing

31. Creating new client welcoming packets

32. Organizing, filing, and typing up notes

33. Planning logistics for events

34. Preparing agendas for meetings

35. Researching products, services, competitors, and current events

36. Sending thank-you , birthday, celebration, sympathy, thinking-of-you cards, and holiday card list

37. Scheduling appointments and managing calendars

38. Social media marketing, designing

39. Solving routine customer issues

40. Sorting e-mails

41. Creating supplies list and maintaining it

42. Tasks that waste your time and talent

43. Transcribing audio recordings and videos

44. Making travel arrangements—Flight, hotel, cars, food, and weather details

45. Web design, updates, and additions

46. Welcoming new clients

47. What you are less qualified for or not good at doing

48. Working with fulfillment house for product

49. Working with and managing vendors

50. Writing instructions for how to perform a task

Don't forget to join us over on Facebook on the Solo to CEO page to pick up some bonus tips and stay connected with us.
www.facebook.com/solotoceo

Many solopreneurs think that in order to be successful, they have to do it the hard way – On Their Own. Now there is a better and more effective way to be successful, and that is delegating and creating a team of people to support you in success.

Imagine if you delegated many of the simple tasks to someone else how it would affect the quality of your life? When you woke up in the morning with less stress and could spend a few extra minutes with your husband before he went off to work. What would it feel like sitting around the family dinner table and truly listen to your kids speak instead of worrying about what else you have to get done before the end of the day? Wouldn't it be nice to take time for yourself and for friends?

This book will help you see the benefits of identifying the everyday tasks that you as the CEO of your company should not be doing, and how to make it simple to delegate so you can stay focused on the important aspects of growing your successful business, and having time for those you care about.

If you are a small business owner, a time pressed parent, an overworked spouse, a new mom or a busy professional, then hiring an assistant will help you create more freedom in your day, save you time, create productivity and make room for you to make a bigger impact in the world.

We will give you the tools to create the necessary systems for you to be a successful entrepreneur and build in the support to help you save time, make more money and have the energy you need to juggle all the balls you have in the air.

You do not get extra points in life by doing it all by yourself. Discover how to give yourself permission to ask for the support you need and want. What are the tasks you can delegate to others so it frees you up to do the important things?

What you have to offer is needed in the world, and it is now time for you to learn to delegate so you can finally claim your title of CEO.

If you'd like us to help, just send an email to: Kimberley@SoloToCEOMentor.com and we will take it from there.

About the Author

Kimberley has been an entrepreneur for 25 years. At the age of 18, she got married to her high school sweetheart. She had a son at 19 and found herself getting divorced at 20. She was a single mom on welfare when she and the guy she was dating started their first company together. Together, they have built five businesses, and she is the CEO in the very first company they started. She is a managing partner in a private security business, a private investigative business, and a security training school. For more than 13 years she has been a business consultant, helping women build solid businesses and bring out their inner CEO so they can expand and discover true business freedom.

Kimberley is an honored recipient of the Small Business Person of the Year award from both the Greater Stockton Chamber of Commerce and the Small Business Administration, Northern California region. She is known as "The Queen of Accountability" because she is committed to helping businesswomen refine their goals, unleash their inner CEO to generate a bigger impact, create massive income results, and attain their dreams while staying true to their values. Kimberley's love for business keeps her constantly moving forward and taking action, and because she is so strong-willed, she can help her clients be resilient and focus on what they are going after.

Kimberley is a co-author of multiple published books, covering such topics as "Partnering Up for Success" and "Welfare to Wealth." She has earned a best-selling book honor as well and a Quilly

Award from the National Academy of Best Selling Authors for her topic "Welfare to Wealth."

She is an owning partner in five thriving businesses with more than 100 employees and a multi-million-dollar budget. She can help you get into action by taking a hobby and turning it into a profitable business or refining a passion and utilizing the strategies she has discovered throughout the years to build solid business foundations. She has worked with top leaders in network marketing companies, as well as many small businesswomen, helping them create organized businesses with lasting structures that grow successfully. She knows what success feels like and helps her clients experience that same feeling.

If that is not enough, she has been married for more than 23 years, has raised four entrepreneur-minded children, and has one adorable grandson.